COLLINS
COBUILD

LEARNER'S
DICTIONARY
WORKBOOK

Bill Mascull

**THE UNIVERSITY
OF BIRMINGHAM**

COLLINS
COBUILD

HarperCollinsPublishers

HarperCollins Publishers
77-85 Fulham Palace Road
London W6 8JB

COBUILD is a trademark of William Collins Sons & Co. Ltd
This edition first published in Great Britain 1996
© HarperCollins Publishers Ltd. 1996

10 9 8 7 6 5 4 3 2 1

ISBN 0 00 375065 5

Designed and typeset by
eMC Design, 2 Grange Lane, Bromham,
Bedfordshire MK43 8NP

Printed and bound by
Caledonian International Book Manufacturing Ltd,
Glasgow, G64

The COBUILD Series

Founding Editor-in-Chief	John Sinclair
Editorial Director	Gwyneth Fox
Editor	Michael Lax
Administration	Michelle Devereux
Illustrations	Ela Bullon
	Anthony Boswell

Corpus Acknowledgements

We would like to acknowledge the assistance of the many
hundreds of individuals and companies who have kindly given
permission for copyright material to be used in The Bank of
English. The written sources include many national and regional
newspapers in Britain and overseas; magazine and periodical
publishers; and book publishers in Britain, the United States and
Australia. Extensive spoken data has been provided by radio
and television broadcasting companies; research workers at
many universities and other institutions; and numerous
individual contributors. We are grateful to them all.

In addition, the author and publisher are grateful to the following for permission to
reproduce the extracts on the pages indicated:

Page 7, John McKie, *The Independent* 6/12/95; page 13 Robin Young, *The Times* 30/6/92, © Times
Newspapers Limited, 1992; page 19, Angella Johnson, © *The Guardian* 18/12/95; page 23, *Today*
13/11/95, © News (UK) Ltd; page 28, Lawrence Donegan, © *The Guardian* 2/6/93; page 32,
Alec Marr, *Today* 5/9/95, © News (UK) Ltd; page 37, David Young, *The Times* 10/8/92, © Times
Newspapers Limited, 1992; page 43 Ian Gallagher, *Today* 30/9/95, © News (UK) Ltd; page 49,
Fran Abrams, *The Independent* 9/1/96; page 54, Duncan Campbell, © *The Guardian* 24/3/93

Note

Introduction

This Workbook is designed to show you the sorts of information you can find in the *Collins COBUILD Learner's Dictionary*, and how to exploit this information to the full.

There are ten units in the Workbook. Each unit contains exercises which cover the following areas, although the titles of the sections in the book are not always the same.

Theme

You learn to use the Dictionary and develop your vocabulary through exercises based on drawings related to different themes such as people, houses, and vehicles.

Frequent word

Perhaps you do not think of looking for very common words like **the** in a dictionary. One of the features of the COBUILD series of dictionaries is that they cover these words in depth. This section of the Workbook will show you what the Dictionary can tell you about these very frequent words.

Grammatical context

The extra column of the Dictionary gives important grammatical information about word classes and grammatical patterns. These are explained in the Grammar section of the Dictionary introduction.

Each unit of the Workbook covers a grammatical word class and will get you into the habit of looking for grammatical information and applying it when you speak and write yourself.

Phrases, idioms, metaphor

Sometimes it is possible to know all the separate words in an expression, but not to understand what the expression means. This section looks in detail at a variety of phrases, idioms, and metaphors; helps you to understand what they mean; and shows you how to find them in the Dictionary.

Pragmatics, register

Some words are always used by a speaker or writer with a particular intention in mind, for example, to show approval or disapproval. These words are indicated by the label PRAGMATICS in a box in the extra column. See the section on Pragmatics in the Dictionary introduction.

Other words are used particularly in British or American English, or are associated with a particular style such as journalism or literature. Again, a label in the extra column of the Dictionary indicates this. See the section on Style and Register in the Dictionary introduction.

A section of each unit of the Workbook deals with these two areas.

Puzzle

This section of each unit of the Workbook encourages you to think about a tricky language area not dealt with in the other sections.

Pronunciation

This section deals, for example, with words that look the same but are pronounced differently, and words that look different but are pronounced the same. Stress is another important issue here, and you will see how to stress words correctly. We also look at differences in pronunciation between British and American English.

Words in context

This section of each unit of the Workbook gives you a number of questions to answer in the context of a newspaper article. The questions are placed next to the part of the article that they refer to, except in Unit 7.

Unit 1

What to wear

Are both women wearing

1 a dress	3 a blouse	5 short sleeves
2 a skirt	4 a brooch	6 high heels?

Formal and casual

1 The man standing up is wearing a
   a suit   b suite   c soot.
2 He is also wearing a
   a skirt and tie   b shirt and tie   c shirt and scarf.
3 Which numbered section of the Dictionary entry
   for **tie** is shown?
   a 2   b 6   c 10.
4 Americans call a tie a
   a tight   b tire   c necktie.
5 Look at the man sitting down. Which numbered
   section of the Dictionary entry for **casual** relates to
   his clothes?
   a 1   b 3   c 4.
6 Which numbered section of the Dictionary entry
   for **casual** relates to his way of sitting?
   a 1   b 2   c 3.
7 Some people might say that his socks and shoes
   are
   a crying   b screaming   c loud.

Formal and formal

1 What is the difference between evening dress and
   an evening dress? Is evening dress the same as
   evening wear? Can men wear evening dress?
2 Is it correct to say that the woman is wearing
   jewellery?
3 Is it correct to say that the woman is wearing her
   hair short?
4 Is it correct to say that the man is wearing a glass?
5 The man is wearing a
   a boa tie   b bow tie   c dinner tie.
6 The man is wearing a
   a dinner jacket   b night jacket   c straitjacket.

Casual and casual

1 Is it correct to say that the person on the left is
   carrying headphones?

2 The person on the left is wearing a
   a tea-shirt   b T-shirt   c tie-shirt.

3 The person on the left is wearing a cap with a
   a pike   b poke   c peak.

4 The person on the right is wearing a
   a jog-suit   b running-suit   c tracksuit.

5 The person on the right is wearing
   a trainees   b trainers   c trailers.

Frequent word: the

Look at the Dictionary entry for **the**. All these examples contain **the**. Which numbered section of the entry for **the** does each example illustrate? (Each example illustrates a different section.)

a When the door opened I couldn't actually see who it was. (___)

b The Italians love fashion in a way the British find hard to understand. (___)

c The rich get richer and the poor get poorer. (___)

d ...Dr Lobstein, author of *Children's Food: The Good, The Bad and The Useless.* (___)

e She was going to take the plane to London. (___)

f They knew that I could sing and play the piano. (___)

g Loosen his clothes at the neck, chest and waist. (___)

h ...Salzburg, perhaps the finest city in Austria. (___)

i Like human beings, well over half the cat's body weight is composed of water. (___)

j The past is a foreign country. They do things differently there. (___)

k To children of the sixties and seventies, classical music was a closed book. (___)

l The more guns you have, the more accidents you're going to have. (___)

Grammatical context: uncount nouns

Uncount nouns are indicated as N-UNCOUNT in the extra column of the Dictionary. This means that they are not usually used in the plural. It is possible to talk about a quantity of something referred to by an uncount noun with a word like 'some' or a phrase like 'a piece of'.

Refer in the Dictionary to the nouns that occur in these sentences and correct the sentences.

1 Can you give me any advices on what to do with it?

2 The company makes everything from aircraft to furnitures and clothes.

3 We've got new uniforms and new equipments. Everything works.

4 Have you got any informations on accommodation in Dublin or Ireland?

5 'I would not like to have been in the traffics.' 'No, I prefer to stay at home.'

6 I look on a car as just a way of getting from A to B. It's just a machinery. It's a box on wheels.

7 Anyone with technical knowledges in the area could have thought of it.

8 American children spend less time in class and do less homeworks than Japanese children.

9 I saw in the press what I thought was a good news.

10 NOTICE TO PASSENGERS. Only one hand baggage allowed inside the aircraft.

Creature expressions

Look at the Dictionary entries for these words:

a cat   c horse   e whale   g worm
b dog   d snail   f wolf

You will see that each entry contains at least one phrase that mentions one of these creatures. Complete the examples using these items.

1 If it was going to be _____ eat _____ , he would do anything it took to get himself re-elected.

2 Hundreds of police failed to prevent travellers from holding music festivals at two sites near Romsey. After a 36-hour game of _____-and-mouse with the police, 2,000 people in 300 vehicles gathered in a disused factory on the edge of town.

3 We were having a marvellous time, a _____ of a time. We saw Edinburgh from top to bottom and had great fun.

4 But this is the old crying _____ thing, isn't it? One day there's going to be a real robbery there.

5 Have you ever tried to drive down the High Street on a Saturday? I have many times. They move at a _____'s pace.

6 Drug abuse is a can of _____s nobody wants to open at sporting events.

7 Most of the book is completely true. 'It comes from the _____'s mouth,' said one friend.

Hey guys

The words in the left column below all refer to people in different ways. Look them up in the Dictionary and say if they:

- can refer to men, women, or both.
- are formal, informal, or neither.
- are British, American, or both.

The first one has been done for you.

	man / woman	formal / informal	British / American
big shot	*both*	*informal*	*both*
bloke			
chap			
character			
guy			
guys			
individual			
personage			

Opposites or what?

The prefix **in-** is added to some adjectives, adverbs, and nouns to form other adjectives, adverbs, and nouns that have the opposite meaning. For example, something that is **incorrect** is not correct.

Look at the definitions of these words beginning **in-** and say what word class they are.

Then look at the word under **Opposite?** Does it have the opposite meaning to the first word, does it have a meaning that is not the opposite, or does it just not exist?

Complete the table by ticking the right boxes. The first three have been done for you.

	Word class			Opposite?	yes	no	does not exist
	adj	adv	noun				
inadequate	✓			adequate	✓		
infamous	✓			famous		✓	
innovation			✓	novation			✓
inaugural				augural			
incessantly				cessantly			
increment				crement			
indolent				dolent			
inflammable				flammable			
influx				flux			
innately				nately			
invaluable				valuable			

Stress and word class 1

When a word belongs to more than one word class, it may be pronounced in different ways. However, this is not always the case. Look at the Dictionary entries for:

- export • import • report • transport

and underline the stressed syllable in these words in each of these examples.

1 If Mexico cannot export its goods, it will export its people.
2 America's imports have been falling and its exports booming.
3 There is no tax on exports and the transport of imports.
4 A master wrote in my school report: 'Teaching this boy is a nightmare.'
5 More than 535 navigation 'incidents' were reported to the Department of Transport last year.

Words in context

Read this article from the *Independent* and answer the questions.

Airborne Mystery of Duchess's Jewels

Police in London and Washington were last night investigating the theft of jewellery believed to be worth £250,000, given to the Duchess of York on her wedding day by the Queen.

The diamond necklace and bracelet were taken from a suitcase belonging to the Duchess's lady-in-waiting, Jane Dunn-Butler, during a flight from New York to London.

Ms Dunn-Butler is thought to have left the suitcase in a baggage hold, from where it was taken. The Duchess discovered the theft late on Monday night after unpacking at her home in Wentworth, Berkshire.

It is not known in which country the items, believed to be royal heirlooms, were stolen, but they were last seen in Washington. Washington police were last night 'having the hotel turned upside down'.

The Duchess arrived home on Monday afternoon after a four-day trip to the US, where she had attended a White House reception hosted by President Bill Clinton and his wife Hillary, and attended a launch for her book *Budgie the Helicopter* at the New York department store, Bloomingdale's. ...

1 Which of these combinations are mentioned in the Dictionary?
   a airborne
   b groundborne
   c waterborne.

2 Would it be possible to use **thieving** instead of **theft** here?

3 What is the normal form of **jewellery** in American English?

4 What is the male equivalent of a duchess?

5 What is the plural of lady-in-waiting?

6 What sort of name is Dunn-Butler?
   a a duo name
   b a bi-name
   c a double-barrelled name.

7 In which sections in the Dictionary are **thought** and **hold** defined as they are used here?

8 Look at the definitions for **heir** and for **loom**. Are heirlooms machines for making cloth for someone's heirs?

9 Where in the Dictionary is this sense of **turn upside down** defined?

10 List all the things that can be attended that are mentioned in sections 1 and 2 of the Dictionary entry for **attend**.

11 List all the things that can be launched that are mentioned in sections 1 to 4 of the Dictionary entry for **launch**.

Unit 2

Mountain scenery

Look at the drawing and complete the sentences with the correct alternatives.
(In some cases, there is more than one correct alternative.)

1 The highest point of a tall mountain is its

  a cap
  b peak
  c summit
  d top.

2 If there is snow on a mountain, you usually say that it is

  a snow-capped
  b snow-peaked
  c snow-summited
  d snow-topped.

3 A glacier is a huge mass of ice that moves very slowly. The related adjective 'glacial' can refer to

  a speed
  b a bad atmosphere between people
  c a man's appearance
  d a woman's appearance.

4 Below the glacier and the waterfall there is a river. In the river you can see large

  a boulders
  b rocks
  c stones
  d pebbles.

5 A section of river where the water moves very fast, often over rocks, is called

  a rapid
  b rapids
  c flows
  d floes.

Features of the landscape

Look at the drawing and complete the sentences with the correct alternatives.
(There is only one correct alternative in each case.)

1 The picture shows a river

  a basin
  b source
  c estuary.

2 In the left foreground there is a

  a march
  b marsh
  c mart.

3 In the marsh, there are

  a reeds
  b reefs
  c riffs.

4 The ship in the river has run

  a abound
  b aground
  c around.

5 In the background there is a

  a lighthouse
  b lightship
  c light industry.

6 In the background there are

  a clefts
  b cleavers
  c cliffs.

Frequent word: a/an

Look at the Dictionary entry for **a/an**. All these examples contain **a** or **an**. Which numbered section of the entry for **a/an** does each example illustrate? (Each example illustrates a different section.)

a I looked over the border and there was a field and a tower with a man with a gun.

(___)

b The competition was won by a Mrs Nora Flynn.

(___)

c Van Gogh said that he couldn't look at a Rembrandt and not believe in God.

(___)

d A man's got to do what a man's got to do.

(___)

e He was an airline pilot, wasn't he?

(___)

f At six on a Saturday evening, the queue for the Hard Rock Cafe goes round the block.

(___)

g He is thought to own a Rolls Royce and a Cadillac.

(___)

h They've got a practical understanding of real-life situations.

(___)

i Take a card, any card.

(___)

j Professor Ericsson said that no amount of chess or music practice would produce a Bobby Fischer or a Mozart.

(___)

Grammatical context: verb patterns 1

Different verbs follow different patterns: look at the section on verb patterns in the introduction to the Dictionary.

Refer in the Dictionary to the entries for the underlined verbs in these badly constructed sentences and correct them. (The relevant section of the entry is shown in brackets.)

Example:

I had to abandon from my very good job with one of the authorities. (1)

If you look at section 1 of the entry for **abandon**, you will see that the pattern is V n, in other words 'verb plus noun' with no words in between. So the sentence should be:

I had to abandon my very good job with one of the authorities.

1 His doctor advised to him to retire as soon as possible. (1)

2 At this point a large dog entered into the room and was told it was not yet lunchtime. (1)

3 Why do you say you hate against shopping? (2)

4 I think I'd like that I go home. (Sub-entry 2, section 6)

5 The Slovaks like wine. The Czechs are preferring beer.

6 The doctor can take these things away, but you can't prevent them to come back. (1)

7 Would you recommend all first-year students to live on campus? (2)

8 I have yet to succeed to make good porridge. (1)

9 I am thinking smokers should respect non-smokers. (1)

Under the weather

Find the meanings of these expressions and say where you can find them in the Dictionary, as in the following example.

If you feel **under the weather**, you
a walk in the rain.
b feel sad because of the weather.
c feel slightly ill.
(The answer is c.
See the entry for **weather**, section 4.)

1 If someone **weathers the storm**, they
  a stay outside during bad weather.
  b reach the end of a very difficult period without much harm or damage.
  c look older because of a very difficult period they have been through.

2 If you say that you are **snowed under**, you
  a are emphasizing that you have a lot of work or other things to deal with.
  b mean that there is a lot of snow under your doorstep or under your car.
  c mean that you are very tired.

3 If you say that you will **take a rain check**, you mean that you
  a will not accept an offer immediately, but that you might accept it later.
  b are going to look outside to see if it is going to rain.
  c are going to cancel a holiday and get your money back because of bad weather.

4 If you say that you **haven't the foggiest**, you are emphasizing that you do not
  a like fog.
  b know something.
  c care what the weather will be like tomorrow.

5 If someone is **under a cloud**,
  a nobody knows where they are.
  b they are feeling ill.
  c people have a poor opinion of them because of something they have done.

The gift of the gab

Look up these items in the Dictionary.

- articulate
- eloquent
- fluent
- gift of the gab
- loquacious
- verbose
- windbag
- wordy

1 Which three words are used to talk about people who express themselves well? Which one of these three words is not used to talk about pieces of writing?

2 Which two words are adjectives used to criticize people who use more words than necessary?

3 Which word is used to describe someone who talks a lot, without necessarily criticizing them for this?

4 Which of these words is formal?

5 Which of these words is rude?

6 What do Americans call the **gift of the gab**?

Sub-entry puzzle

Some words, of course, can have several unrelated meanings. Entries for these words in the Dictionary are divided into separate sub-entries. Use the clues to find the sub-entry and section numbers of the words below, as in the following example.

can

a a modal verb meaning that someone has the ability or opportunity to do something. (Sub-entry 1, section 2)

b a metal container in which something such as food or drink is put. (2 , 1)

c an expression containing **can** meaning that you have to take all the blame for something. (2 , 4)

1 **down**

a used with verbs to talk about travelling to a place, perhaps one to the south. (__ , __)

b used to talk about machines that are not working. (__ , __)

c used to talk about someone who is unhappy. (__ , __)

2 **fancy**

a a noun meaning a liking or a desire for someone or something. (__ , __)

b an adjective used to describe things that are very expensive. (__ , __)

c used in an expression with **take** to talk about things that people start liking, perhaps for no reason. (__ , __)

3 **give**

a used with nouns like **concert** to talk about public performances. (__ , __)

b used to talk about having an object in your hands and then passing it to someone so that they have it in their hands. (__ , __)

c used to talk about something that breaks, for example because there is too much weight on it. (__ , __)

4 **mean**

a a verb used to talk about what someone is referring to or intending to say. (__ , __)

b an adjective used to criticize people who do not like spending money. (__ , __)

c an adjective used to describe places that are poor. (__ , __)

5 **train**

a a sequence of events. (__ , __)

b another word for **teach**, used to talk about teaching skills. (__ , __)

c used with **on** to talk about aiming guns in a particular direction. (__ , __)

Same spelling, different pronunciations

Several words have different pronunciations when they are used with different meanings or in different ways. After each example there are possible rhymes for the word in bold. Underline the word in brackets that the word in bold rhymes with.

1 Do you think as many people would use **lead**-free petrol if it was the same price as leaded? (red / reed)
I don't **lead** such an exciting life that I don't know where I'm going to be. (head / heed)

2 Obviously he's dressed up. He's gone out and bought a **bow**-tie. (hoe / how)
You're supposed to **bow** your head in prayer, but I just couldn't do it. (crow / cow)

3 ...the hotels that line the Pacific shore at Acapulco like a **row** of teeth. (know / now)
It was the classic case of the dinner party where the invited couple is invited so that the married couple can have a **row**. (now / note)

4 The incident with McMahon had brought blood from his nose and **tears** to his eyes. (fears / fares)
Fifty thousand lecturers are being asked to **tear** up a professional contract. (rear / rare)

5 It's much too late now to **wind** back the clock to a year ago. (signed / sinned)
The sun shone all morning; there was the music of **wind** in the trees. (binned / bind)

Words in context

Read this article from *The Times* and answer the questions.

Ponytail man claims sex bias

A ponytailed man who was dismissed from his job for refusing to have his hair cut claimed yesterday that he was the victim of sexual discrimination because women employees were allowed long hair.

Kevin Lloyd, 36, left his job as a computer engineer after being ordered to trim his hair, which reached halfway down his back, or to find a new job. The ultimatum came when his employer, Allied Software, told Mr Lloyd that his haircut clashed with the company image. Brian Wizard, customer services director, told the tribunal: 'He indicated that he had always worn his hair like that. I said if he wasn't prepared to have his hair cut, I would be terminating his employment.'

Mr Lloyd, of Wapping, East London, said he refused the request on principle. Clients were interested only in his technical knowledge. 'There was no one who said to me, "You can solve my computer problem but first get your hair cut".' He is claiming unfair dismissal and sexual discrimination against Allied Software of Slough, Berkshire. The hearing continues today.

1 Which syllable in **bias** is the one that is usually stressed?

2 If someone is dismissed from their job, do they leave it because they want to?

3 Which of the three definitions of **discrimination** in the Dictionary relates to the discrimination referred to here?

4 **Trim** is another word for _ _ _ .

5 Which prepositions are used after **halfway** in the examples of **halfway** in the Dictionary?

6 An ultimatum is a form of
w _ _ _ _ _ _ .

7 Is this the same sort of tribunal as the one mentioned in the example in the Dictionary in the entry for **tribunal**?

8 Is it possible to spell principle, as it used here, as **principal**?

9 Is it possible to talk about technical **knowledges**?

10 Which of the five definitions of **hearing** in the Dictionary relates to the hearing referred to here?

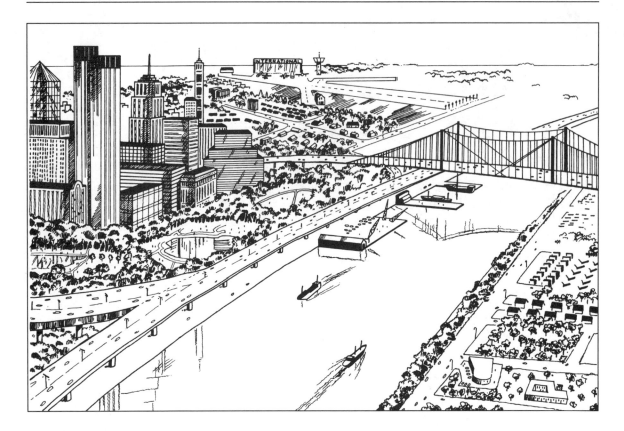

Possible urban combinations

Which of these compounds and combinations are possible, and which are incorrect?
Cross out the impossible combinations, as shown.

downtown	~~sidetown~~	~~centretown~~	~~off-town~~
tower block	blocktower	house block	office block
hanging bridge	hung bridge	suspended bridge	suspension bridge
high street	fly road	down road	elevated highway
aerodrome	airfield	airport	airstrip
dockland	quayside	quayhouse	warehouse

Now just look at the possible combinations. Tick (✔) the ones that refer to things in the picture.

Olde Worlde charm

Underline the right alternative in each case.

This is a *view / outlook / oversight* over the *ceilings / roofs / rooves* of an old town. The town looks *mediaval / medieval / medievil*. The church has a tall *tour / towel / tower* with a *spiral / spire / squire* on top. In the *backdrop / background / backlog*, there are trees and other churches.

There are two main streets and off these run smaller, narrow *whining / winding / wining* streets. In one of the main streets, there is a traffic *freeze / hold-all / jam*. This street suffers a lot from traffic *congestion / crowds / stoppages*. In the other, traffic is *banned / disallowed / prevented* and *footmen / pedestrians / walkmen* can go shopping without the danger of being run over. But *parking / standing / stationing* is difficult, and some people prefer to do their shopping *out-town / out of town / outdoors town*.

Frequent word: be

Look at the Dictionary entry for **be**. It has these sub-entries:

1 auxiliary verb uses
2 other verb uses.

Which sub-entry does each underlined example illustrate, and which numbered section does it relate to? (Each example illustrates a different section.)

a I was expected to do extremely well in English.

(__ , __)

b Holcroft began to develop a number of themes that he was to use later on.

(__ , __)

c Charlie is not himself. I think he is lonely in the flat.

(__ , __)

d The thing is he's now doing a full-time job.

(__ , __)

e They play some of the best dance music to be heard anywhere in the world.

(__ , __)

f What is to be done about the private car?

(__ , __)

g We encouraged her to be herself and did not put her under any pressure.

(__ , __)

h I don't know what the clubs can do about it to be honest.

(__ , __)

i You could almost forgive Madonna if you thought she was sad. But she's not. She's as happy as can be.

(__ , __)

j It's nice that you can still smile about it.

(__ , __)

Grammatical context: phrasal verb patterns

Look at the phrasal verb patterns on pages xvi and xvii of the Grammar section in the Dictionary introduction. Then look at section 1 of the entry for **look up** in the Dictionary itself.

You will see that the pattern with **look up** can be

- V n P: verb+noun+particle
- V P noun: verb+particle+noun, *but not* verb+particle+pronoun.

So it is possible to say:

Look the word up in the dictionary.
Look it up in the dictionary.
Look up the word in the dictionary.

but not:

~~Look up it in the dictionary.~~

Check the missing particle in the Dictionary, and change the word order of the following sentences, as in the following example.

Add the figures _____ to get the total.
Add the figures up to get the total.
Add them up to get the total.
Add up the figures to get the total.

1 People are free to choose how to bring _____ their children.

2 The police had to check _____ the call.

3 The agriculture minister has tried to explain _____ the scandal.

4 We flagged _____ the tractor and climbed aboard.

5 I'll never be able to give _____ smoking.

6 I marked _____ the number on a scrap of paper.

7 They narrowed _____ the choice to about a dozen sites.

8 The enemy claimed to have shot _____ 22 of our planes.

9 Women need to weigh _____ the risks.

Watery phrases

The expressions in bold can be used in connection with water,
but here they are used in connection with other things.
Check them in the Dictionary and match the two parts of the sentences.

1 Former Yugoslavia

2 Though the document remains officially confidential,

3 'He had captured her magical looks at a magical moment.'

4 We should not be blind

5 The president faced a **torrent** of questions

6 Foreign money is **trickling**, not **flooding**, into the region

7 It's easy now to look at the situation and say we might have done this or might have done that,

a but it's **water under the bridge** now.

b but will never **trickle down** to most firms.

c on the Whitewater affair.

d to the **rising tide** of racism.

e His biographical style can be equally **gushing**.

f **ebbs and flows** in the headlines.

g it has been extensively **leaked**.

Everything in common but their language 1

Find the equivalents of these terms relating to buildings in the other variety of English.
The first one has been done for you.

British English	American English
car park	parking lot
caretaker	
	elevator
	first floor
flat	
tap	
	closet
	drapes
estate agent	
	burglarize

What is there to see?

Look at the Dictionary entries for the words in bold
and complete the information about them, following
the example of **landscape**.

	countryside	landscape	scenery	seascape
What you can see around you in a town		✔		
What you can see around you in the country		✔		
Theatre equipment				
A type of painting		✔		
All the features that are important in a particular situation		✔		
What people do to land to create a pleasing effect		✔		

Unlikely couples

Aloud is pronounced the same as another word: **allowed**. In the sentences below,
there are other similar pairs. Find the word missing in the second sentence of each pair,
as in the example. Check the Dictionary for pronunciation and spelling.

I always read my stuff <u>aloud</u> when I'm writing.
People are not <u>allowed</u> to smoke on buses and trains.

1 He has always sounded like a one-man <u>band</u>.

   Drivers are _____ from using their cars one
   day a week.

2 The resulting fire and explosion <u>blew</u> the roof off.

   Clinton stopped at a picnic for 7,000 people under
   _____ skies in Orlando.

3 Crime can pay, even if you are <u>caught</u>.

   No one dances on a tennis _____ like
   Nastase.

4 They eat good simple food: beans, rice, <u>flour</u> and
   maize.

   I think daffodils are a beautiful _____ .

5 Any idiot could have <u>guessed</u> he'd do this.

   I felt I was a _____ in this country.

6 The crowd roared itself <u>hoarse</u>.

   Never look a gift _____ in the mouth.

7 ...the riverside <u>quays</u> of Rouen and Le Havre.

   Too many farmers still leave the _____ in
   their tractors overnight.

8 He designed his own <u>pair</u> of boots and test-walked
   them in the desert.

   There were lots of apple trees and _____
   trees.

9 ... <u>raw</u> materials such as oil, wood and metals.

   You could hear the _____ of traffic from the
   road across the forest.

Words in context

Read this article from the *Guardian* and answer the questions.

Antarctic Walker Forced to Quit

Angella Johnson on a technical hitch

Explorer Roger Mear has been forced by the failure of vital equipment to abandon his attempted record-breaking solo walk across Antarctica after only six weeks.

This leaves the way clear for Norwegian challenger Borge Ousland, aged 33, to try to complete the 1,700-mile trek. He began it on November 11, a week after Mear, aged 45, had set out to become the first person to walk alone and unsupported across the continent. …

Hopes that he would walk into the record books ended at 11.58 GMT on Saturday when his satellite beacon sent a distress signal to a rescue centre in Plymouth: 'I have an emergency, please get me out.'

It gave his position as 800 miles from the South Pole. A Twin Otter aircraft with two guides and a doctor left Patriot Hills in the Antarctic, spotted his tent and airlifted him to safety at 21.00 GMT.

Although Mear has been reported as physically fit, a statement from the expedition team says equipment failure meant the explorer would have been in a life-threatening situation if not found in a few hours. The explorer is expected to return to his Derbyshire home for Christmas. …

1 If something is vital, is it very important?

2 Which word in this paragraph means the same as one in the headline?

3 If you do something solo, you do it
a _ _ _ _ .

4 What record is Ousland a challenger for?

5 A trek is a journey, but can it be an easy journey?

6 Which two of the four meanings of **set out** in the Dictionary could apply here?

7 Which numbered section of the entry for **record** does this relate to?

8 Which syllable of **distress** is stressed?

9 If you spot someone or something, do you
a note them
b notice them
c notate them?

10 If equipment fails, it stops working
p _ _ _ _ _ _ _ .

11 Does **life-threatening** have a separate entry in the Dictionary?

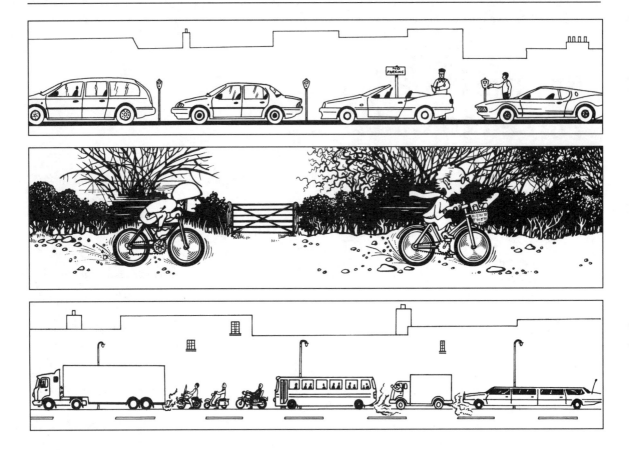

Vehicle jungle

Some of these vehicles are in the drawings and some are not. Tick (✔) the ones that are.

coach   limousine   push bike
convertible   lorry   saloon car
double-decker   moped   scooter
estate car   motorbike   sports car
hansom cab   mountain bike   van
hatchback   penny farthing

In the Dictionary, which of these words are labelled BRITISH and which are labelled DATED?
Label the words 'B' and 'D' respectively.

Frequent word: of

Look at the Dictionary entry for **of**. All these examples contain **of**.
Which numbered section of the entry for **of** does each example illustrate?
(Each example illustrates a different section.)

a He said the song was 'a shout of pain and protest'.
  (___)

b The proposed height of the Saguling dam was
  lowered by five metres. (___)

c You know I like a glass of wine when I'm doing the
  cooking. (___)

d Philip Larkin was afraid of death. (___)

e It reminded her of Paris nightclubs in the
  Twenties. (___)

f Food is less of a problem than might be expected.
  (___)

g Take a clean sheet of paper. (___)

h Hammurabi, King of Babylon, brought in laws that
  limited doctors' fees. (___)

i His grip is of iron. (___)

j The birth of Jesus may have been as early as 8 BC.
  (___)

k It's very nice of you to have me on the programme.
  (___)

l I thought I had remained a semi-young man of 35.
  (___)

Grammatical context: plurals

What are the plurals of these nouns? Divide them into six logical groups
according to the way their plurals are formed. Explain the basis for each group.
(There are at least two words in each group.)

singular	plural	singular	plural	singular	plural
aircraft		leaf		spacecraft	
criterion		passer-by		thief	
foot		phenomenon		tomato	
goose		potato		tooth	
hanger-on		sheep		wolf	

Group 1	Group 2	Group 3
Why?	Why?	Why?

Group 4	Group 5	Group 6
Why?	Why?	Why?

Out of control

Look in the Dictionary at the entries for the words in bold and say which metaphors relate to:

- cars
- planes
- ships
- trains

One of the metaphors relates to planes or ships and one relates to planes or cars. (For 1, look also at the entries for **tail** and for **spin** to get extra clues.)

1 President Clinton set up a special commission to study the airlines' problems and help pull the airlines out of their financial **tailspin**.
2 With Vaclav Havel's decision to leave the **helm**, the government now looks well and truly sunk.
3 The state government of Arizona is like the kid who stole his parents' car and is out **careering** into other people's lawns, crashing into garbage cans and running red lights.
4 The rising violence will not **derail** the peace talks.
5 ...the England team, minus their captain and apparently **rudder**less.
6 The governing body of international motor racing, FISA, has put a new man in the **driving seat**.

Approving and disapproving of people

These words are used to talk about people's characters and attitudes. Look them up in the Dictionary and put 'A' against those that show approval and 'D' against those that show disapproval.

apathetic ___   philistine ___

brash ___   pompous ___

cool-headed ___   simple-minded ___

dynamic ___   strong-minded ___

easy-going ___   sulky ___

modest ___   tactful ___

narcissistic ___   thoughtful ___

obsequious ___

Work puzzle

Look in the Dictionary at the entries and examples for these words and answer the questions about them.

- chore
- occupation
- post
- task
- job
- position
- profession
- work

1 Is it possible to talk about **a work** when talking about a job?
2 Are **jobs for the boys** done by boys?
3 Is it possible to say that someone **resigns their post** if they leave a job?
4 Which numbered section of the entry for **position** refers to the meaning **job**?
5 Can **profession** refer to any kind of job?
6 Does **occupation** always refer to a job?
7 If you **take someone to task**, do you ask them to do some work?
8 A **chore** is a kind of task, but can it be pleasant or interesting?

Stress and word class 2

The words in bold are stressed differently according to their word class. Check them in the Dictionary and underline the stressed syllable in each of them.

1 ...laporoscopes, which can be used to **conduct** operations without cutting the body open.
2 They have a lot of family **conflict** and decisions have to be made.
3 Devedzija learnt about radios as a **conscript** in the army.
4 The men have 24 hours to **construct** a 500-seat theatre.
5 The Ryder Cup, once **contested** between America, Britain and Ireland, since 1979 has been America versus Europe.
6 **Contrast** this peaceful atmosphere with the situation last year.
7 ...Fatma, a German woman married to a Turk and a **convert** to Islam.
8 The police use video cameras to **convict** drivers of speeding offences.

Words in context

Read this article from *Today* and answer the questions.

Reptiles Loose on Jet

by Today Reporter

Exotic reptiles, including pythons, lizards and scorpions sparked panic when they escaped from a cargo crate on a passenger jet.

Staff only discovered the creepy crawlies were on the loose when cargo handlers at Manchester Airport opened the door of the hold – and quickly shut it again.

The British Airways Boeing 757 was immediately taken out of service until a reptile expert arrived to round up the escapees. ...

But British Airways said there was no need to worry, even though there were 703 reptiles on board the 90-minute shuttle flight from London.

'None of the reptiles was poisonous so there is no need for passengers on the flight to worry about snakes or other creepy crawlies in their luggage,' said a spokesman. 'The passengers' luggage was in a separate compartment.'...

The consignment, in five crates and destined for a Manchester dealer, had been checked by customs on arrival from Ghana.

1 Which types of reptile are mentioned in the definition of **reptile** in the Dictionary?

2 Which numbered section of the entry for **spark** is this an example of?

3 A crate is a large b _ _ .

4 Who normally uses the expression **creepy crawly**?

5 Which numbered section of the entry for **loose** is this an example of?

6 Which animals are mentioned in the example for **round up** in the Dictionary?

7 Does a shuttle service go to lots of different places?

8 What four-letter word is used earlier in the article for a compartment on a plane?

9 A consignment of goods is a l _ _ _ that is being delivered to one place.

10 What is the official name for the customs organization in Britain given in the Dictionary?

Dream homes

Match these words to their definitions. Which of these homes are in the drawing?

1 bungalow

2 cabin

3 chalet

4 cottage

5 detached house

6 residence

7 semi

8 shack

9 terraced house

10 villa

a fairly large house, especially one used for holidays in Mediterranean countries

b formal word for the place someone lives. Not a particular type of building

c house with only one storey

d house joined to another house on one side by a shared wall

e old or flimsy hut built from tin, wood, or other materials

f small house, especially in the country

g small wooden house in an area of forests or mountains. 'Log' often comes in front of this word

h small wooden house, especially in a mountain area or holiday camp

i independent house not joined to other houses

j a house that is one of a row of similar houses

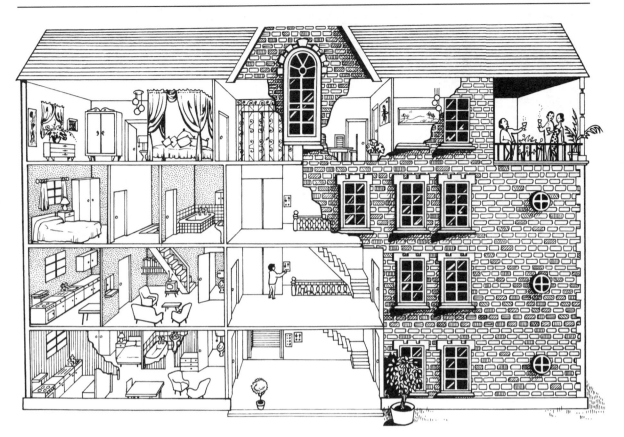

An estate agent speaks

A British estate agent is talking about a building where there are flats to rent.
Are the statements true or false? If a statement is false, say why.

1 This building has got four floors and a flat roof.

2 All the flats are on two floors.

3 Every flat has a balcony.

4 The lift goes to every floor. On the top floor, there are special gates outside the lift doors.

5 Some of the flats are unfurnished.

6 All the flats are unoccupied.

7 Every flat has a hall that you go through to get to the other rooms.

8 There are wardrobes in every bedroom.

9 There are curtains over all the windows.

10 In the first floor flat, there is a staircase that leads directly up into the bedroom.

Frequent word: and

Look at the Dictionary entry for **and**. All these examples contain **and**.
Which numbered section of the entry for **and** does each example illustrate?
(Each example illustrates a different section.)

a They forced a man out of his car and drove away.
   (___)

b They thought I was David Niven. And they still call me David Niven to this day. (___)

c John and I took up skiing after we gave up athletics. (___)

d I'd been asked if I'd like to do this job. So we discussed it and in the end decided that I should. (___)

e Around 125mm of rain was reported and the River Avon at Bath rose six feet during the afternoon. (___)

f He was just fifty and a half when this happened. (___)

g Three and two make five. (___)

h I wish that we could have stayed married for ever and ever. (___)

i Branson sells Virgin record label for five hundred and ten million pounds. (___)

j 'We no longer have the means to make war, we must make peace to win.' 'And now?' (___)

Grammatical context: adjectives

Look at the adjective patterns on page xix of the Grammar section in the Dictionary introduction.
Look in the extra column of the Dictionary at the word class labels for these adjectives and divide them into three groups, those that:

1 can be graded.
2 can never be graded.
3 can sometimes be graded and sometimes ungraded, depending on different uses corresponding to different numbered sections of the definition.

	group		group		group
ablaze		affable		ambidextrous	
abnormal		afraid		amphibious	
absent		alight		anatomical	
adrift		alive		asleep	
advisable		alone		awake	

Disaster area

The words in bold in the sentences 1-7 are also used to talk about disasters. Look up the words in the Dictionary and relate them to the types of disaster a-g.

a collapsed building
b earthquake
c fast-moving water
d fire
e not enough rain
f nuclear accident
g strong wind and rain

1 In October 1990, Hatton was arrested in a **blaze** of publicity and taken to the police station.

2 After the 44th move, Spassky's position was in **ruins.**

3 There is a good deal of violence in Dempsy but 'only' 41 killings in six months, which, as one of the city's cops says, is not exactly a **tidal wave** of blood.

4 Lorenzo scored after half an hour, ending a long goal **drought** for Swindon.

5 Dire Straits took London by **storm** last night in the first of six concerts at Earl's Court.

6 The techniques of the cinema change slowly, but from time to time a major **tremor** shakes them. Such a tremor was *Terminator 2.*

7 Last year people were predicting a terrible **meltdown** in the air traffic control system.

Literary people

The nouns 1-10 are labelled LITERARY in the extra column of the Dictionary. This means that they are only usually used in literary writing. Match them to their everyday equivalents, a-j.

	a criminal, or someone who has
1 bard	behaved badly
2 comrade	b poet
3 crone	c male relative
4 cuckold	d unhappy or unfortunate person
5 kinsman	e old woman
6 maiden	f friend
7 miscreant	g man whose wife is having an
8 sage	affair with another man
9 victor	h winner
10 wretch	i wise person
	j young woman

Talking about the future

Correct these sentences. There is one word too many in each of them. (Look at the Dictionary entries in brackets for clues.)

1 The marriage of Alix and Bertie appeared to be on to the brink of disaster. (**brink**)

2 There's every chance that something better will be around of the corner if she does the sensible thing. (**corner**, section 7)

3 Was there no good news to on the horizon? (**horizon**, section 3)

4 A final victory over the Mafia is possible. Possible, maybe, but not in imminent. (**imminent**)

5 Are you going to get a computer in the near to future? (**near**, section 15)

6 The huge factory was on the point at of beginning production of one million television sets. (**point**, section 14)

7 Those changes still seem at a long way away. (**way**, section 25)

Fertile exercise

These words are pronounced differently in British and American English.
Look them up in the Dictionary and divide them into three logical groups of four words each.
Explain the basis for each group.

adult	fertile	hostile	laboratory	nude	tune
amateur	futile	institute	moustache	numerical	volatile

Group 1	Group 2	Group 3
Why?	Why?	Why?

Words in context

Read this article from the *Guardian* and answer the questions.

Tenners from Heaven

by Lawrence Donegan

Consider yesterday's events in Beaumont Road, Bolton. James Woods, aged 23, left home at 8.55am to deliver a carrier bag containing the takings from his father's chemist's shop to the bank.

He placed the bag on the roof of his car, climbed inside and drove off. As the cash fluttered down on to Beaumont Road in the early morning rush hour, all human life unfolded.

Pain: Greater Manchester Police said last night the bag contained 'several thousand pounds'. Mr Woods, said by friends to be 'very upset', said afterwards: 'I simply put the bag on top of the car and forgot about it. I didn't realise about the cash until I got to the bank.'

Greed: Eye-witnesses said that within minutes of Mr Woods driving off, 60 people were running across the road trying to gather five- and ten-pound notes as they fell to the ground.

Danger: Beaumont Road has a 60mph speed limit.

Satisfaction: One motorist who was driving to his office in Bolton said he stopped at the scene because he thought there had been a road accident. 'I asked one bloke who owned the money. He said "Who cares. It's Christmas." He was stuffing notes into a bag; he must have picked up thousands.' John Bailey of nearby Meridan Grove, said: 'One man told me his wife had picked up about £300.'

Compassion: Police said a local solicitor had been passing and watched the events unfold. 'He obtained a list of the registration numbers of these vehicles,' a spokesman said.

Remorse: Mr Woods, of Lostock, said that by mid-morning £360 had been handed in to Bolton police. 'My father doesn't know yet. He's gone shopping.'

Menace: 'We expect the rest of the money to be eventually handed in once drivers realise their numbers were taken,' the police spokesman added. 'It is our intention to visit their homes and get the money back.'

1 A tenner is a ten-pound note and a fiver is a five-pound note. Is a 'twentier' a twenty-pound note?

2 What do you normally put in a carrier bag?

3 Do American shopkeepers talk about the **takings** of their shop?

4 Which numbered section of the entry for **place** in the Dictionary is this an example of?

5 Can heavy objects flutter down?

6 Does the rush hour last an hour?

7 When a situation unfolds, it
   d _ _ _ _ _ _ _ .

8 Which numbered section of the entry for **upset** in the Dictionary is this an example of?

9 What is the adjective corresponding to **greed**?

10 If you are an eye-witness to an event, you see it h _ _ _ _ _ _ .

11 What does **mph** stand for?

12 If you stuff something into a bag, do you put it in the bag slowly and gently?

13 Do solicitors exist in the American legal system?

14 What is the equivalent of **spokesman** that can refer to both men and women?

15 If you feel remorse about something, do you feel guilty about it?

16 A menace is a t h r _ _ _ _ .

17 If something happens eventually, does it happen immediately?

Unit 6

True, false, or worse?

Look at the drawing of the living room.
- Which of these statements are true?
- Which are false?
- Which are impossible from the language point of view?

(Some of the statements have more than one thing wrong with them.)

1 There are not many furnitures.
2 There is wall-to-wall carpeting.
3 There is parquet flooring.
4 There is a rugg in front of the fireplace.
5 There are two lazy chairs next to the rug.
6 There are four eating chairs around the eating table.
7 There are hi-fi equipments on the shelfs.
8 There is a low coffee table on the rug.
9 The rug has a fridge around its edge.
10 There are French windows opposite to the shelves.

Design for living

The table on the right has 16 expressions. Cross out the ones that cannot be used to describe a room, as shown. Then look at both drawings and tick the expressions that accurately describe them, as shown.

The room is ...	Living room	Kitchen	The room is ...	Living room	Kitchen
a dump		✓	impeccable		
a mess			neat		
a pigsty			ordered		
a tip			orderly		
clean			smart		
~~clean-cut~~			tidy		
disorganized			well-dressed		
immaculate			workmanlike		

Frequent word: that

Look at the Dictionary entry for **that**. It has these sub-entries:

1 demonstrative uses
2 conjunction and relative pronoun uses.

Which sub-entry does each example illustrate, and which numbered section does it relate to?

(Each example illustrates a different section.)

a Later that year she sailed to England and settled in a flat in Mayfair.
(__ , __)

b 'Was it Buffalo Bill?' 'Yeah, that's it.'
(__ , __)

c The weather was so bad that the aircraft were not used for long.
(__ , __)

d It's amazing that the Italians and the French turn out so many good cyclists.
(__ , __)

e Well, when I got married I stood on my own feet and that was it.
(__ , __)

f We're supposed to learn about the Redcoats and George Washington and all that.
(__ , __)

g Try looking at that picture over there.
(__ , __)

h We can't get rid of him just like that.
(__ , __)

i It probably took her all day and a good hard day at that.
(__ , __)

j Raising the cash to buy a boat is not that difficult.
(__ , __)

Grammatical context: adverbs

Some of these words may look like adverbs, but are not adverbs. Others may not look like adverbs, but are. Which are adverbs, which are adjectives, and which both? Indicate this in the table. The first one has been done for you.

	adverb	adjective
awfully	✔	
comely		
fast		
friendly		
hard		
hardly		
heavenly		
homely		
incredibly		
motley		
perfectly		
prettily		
quarterly		
really		
reasonably		

Colourful expressions

Which of these expressions is the odd one out and why?

black box	yellow flower
brownstone	grey area
red herring	green belt
blue ribbon	white elephant

Jargon jungle

These terms, or certain uses of them, are labelled TECHNICAL in the Dictionary. The definition gives the area in which each word is used. Match the words 1–11 with the areas a–k.

1 acceleration	a anthropology
2 caries	b biology
3 Caucasian	c business
4 collocate	d computing
5 dorsal	e dentistry
6 fugue	f electronics
7 liquidate	g linguistics
8 matrix	h mathematics
9 precipitation	i meteorology
10 resistor	j music
11 shareware	k physics

Confusable adjectives

Check the alternatives a-c in the Dictionary and complete the sentences correctly.

1 If you are not interested in what you are doing, or have nothing to do, you are
   a bored   b boring   c uninteresting.

2 Someone no longer living is
   a dead   b death   c died.

3 Things that may happen, but are not certain to happen are
   a eventual   b final   c possible.

4 Something that is very tiring is
   a exhausting b exhaustive c extenuating.

5 Mr Smith has recently died. You can refer to him as the _____ Mr Smith.
   a former   b last   c late

6 If something attracts your attention, it is
   a interested   b interesting c interestive.

7 If someone is sad that there is no one with them, they feel
   a alone   b lone   c lonely.

8 If you understand other people's needs, you are
   a sensed   b sensible   c sensitive.

9 Someone who is friendly and pleasant is
   a kind   b nice   c sympathetic.

10 Something very valuable is
   a costless   b priceless   c worthless.

Stress in compounds 1

Look up these words in the Dictionary and indicate which are stressed on the first syllable and which on the first and the second. The first one has been done for you.

	first syllable stressed	first and second syllables stressed
backcloth	✔	
backcomb		
backdate		
back door		
backfire		
background		
backhander		
backlash		
back pedal		
backstroke		
backtrack		
backup		

Words in context

Read this article from *Today* and answer the questions.

Boy cracks dad's safe to go on Disney spree
He blew £7,000 in 10 days

by Alec Marr in Paris

He was a real big spender. Booking in at the best hotel. Casually peeling off the 500-franc notes. ...

To the management of Disneyland Paris he was a very welcome guest. Even though he was only 12 years old. In the end security officials became suspicious. They called the police. And discovered that the schoolboy was living the high life on £10,000 nicked from his father's safe.

The boy, named only Lamine, had disappeared from the family hotel in Paris 10 days earlier. While police all over France searched for him, he was living it up at a £250-a-night Disneyland hotel.

He went on all the rides and went on every other attraction in the place.

Enough

And when he'd had enough of Disneyland for a while, he paid £650 to hire a six-door chauffeured limousine to take him to neighbouring Asterix Park for a day.

Then he was driven back to Disneyland, where he treated new-found friends to expensive rides. By the time he was rumbled, Lamine had got through £7,000 of his father's money. ...

1 If someone goes on a spree, do they behave in a reasonable way?

2 Which meaning of the Dictionary entry for **safe** is used here?

3 Do Americans talk about **booking in** to a hotel?

4 If you do something casually, do you look as though you are nervous?

5 If someone becomes suspicious, do they become suspect?

6 **Nick** is an informal word for s _ _ _ _ _ .

7 If you live it up, do you have a quiet time?

8 Which meaning of the Dictionary entry for **attraction** is used here?

9 Are limousines normally driven by chauffeurs?

10 Which meaning of the Dictionary entry for **treat** is used here?

11 If someone is rumbled, is something good discovered about them?

The usual suspects

Match the descriptions to the suspects in this police line-up.

a Below average height, overweight, balding, moustache. (___)

b Above average height, scrawny build, totally bald, clean-shaven. (___)

c Average height, short hair, clean-shaven, glasses, average build with round shoulders. (___)

d Average height, clean-shaven, stocky, balding, paunch. (___)

e Above average height, dishevelled, thin, long beard, long hair. (___)

f Above average height, muscular build, crew cut, clean-shaven. (___)

Frequent word: have

Look at the Dictionary entry for **have**. It has these sub-entries:

1 auxiliary verb uses
2 with nouns describing actions
3 other verb uses and phrases
4 modal phrases.

Which sub-entry does each example illustrate, and which numbered section does it relate to?
(Each example illustrates a different section.)

a 'I have just been to the garage,' she said.

(__ , __)

b She was extremely nervous, having just seen a man shot outside her flat.

(__ , __)

c They've got another dog now, haven't they?

(__ , __)

d Did you have a shower or a bath?

(__ , __)

e One of my friends has a big beard.

(__ , __)

f You're just lucky if you haven't had flu.

(__ , __)

g *Flica* was sold to an Italian owner who is having the yacht repaired.

(__ , __)

h He ran out and got into a car that had the door open.

(__ , __)

i Legend has it that he made his fortune in the 1950s.

(__ , __)

j Yoko had to leave class halfway through.

(__ , __)

Grammatical context: verb patterns 2

Look at the section on ergative verbs, labelled V-ERG, on page xv of the Grammar section in the Dictionary introduction. Then look in the Dictionary at the entries for the verbs in bold in the questions, and answer the questions.

If you

1 **shake** a tree, does the tree shake?

2 **shape** an object, does the object shape?

3 **shatter** a window, does the window shatter?

4 **shrink** a garment when you wash it, does the garment shrink?

5 **spin** a coin, does the coin spin?

6 **splice** two pieces of rope together, does the rope splice?

7 **spot** someone, for example in a crowd, does the person spot?

8 **sprain** your ankle, does your ankle sprain?

9 **staple** some sheets of paper together, do the sheets staple?

10 **start** an engine, does the engine start?

11 **stick** two things together, do the two things stick?

12 **stress** a point in a discussion, does the point stress?

Questions of life

Where in the Dictionary can you find the definitions of these expressions?
Write down which come under the main headword for **life**, and which come under other headwords.

	headword
double life	
get a life	
kiss of life	
larger than life	
life and soul of the party	
long-life	
shelf life	
still life	
That's life	
the time of your life	

Everything in common but their language 2

Find the equivalents of these terms relating to vehicles in the other variety of English.
The first one has been done for you.

British English	American English
boot	trunk
	hood
estate car	
	tailpipe
lorry	
petrol	
	sedan
tyre	
windscreen	
wing	

Confusable nouns

Check the alternatives a-c in the Dictionary and complete the sentences correctly.

1 When you go from one place to another on land, you go on a
a travel   b journey   c voyage.

2 The thing that produces power in a jet plane is called
a a motor   b an engine   c a machine.

3 Scientists do
a experiences   b expertises   c experiments.

4 Things you buy on holiday to remind you of the place you visited are
a memories   b memoirs   c souvenirs.

5 The money that someone gets for giving information to the police about a crime is
a an award   b a reward   c a recompense.

6 A report in a newspaper in which someone gives their opinion of a book or concert is a
a critic   b criticism   c review.

7 Someone who belongs to a country that is not your own is
a a foreigner   b a stranger   c an abroader.

8 If you give your opinion or make a statement about something, you make a
a comment   b commentary   c mention.

Same or different 1

Check the pronunciation of these pairs of words in the Dictionary.
Look especially at different meanings, and pronunciation in British and American English.
Are the underlined vowel sounds the same:

- always
- never
- sometimes: if so when?

Indicate this information in the table. Two have been done for you.

	always	never	sometimes: when?
bare / bear	✔		
deliberate / estimate			
head / read			when **read** is the past tense
kind / wind			
now / sow			
paw / saw			
pear / pier			
realize / surprise			

Words in context

Read this article from *The Times* and check the
Dictionary to find the correct words to complete the
sentences. (The number of letters in each word is
given in brackets.)

Four killed as storms batter Britain
by David Young

Four people died as violent storms
crossed Britain yesterday. Torrential rain
and lightning caused fires, flooding and
traffic disruption. Thousands of homes
in Lincolnshire and Northamptonshire
lost power supplies and six houses in
Northamptonshire were set on fire by
lightning. A Northampton fire station
was also hit by lightning, suffering
damage to communications equipment.
In Kettering houses in three streets were
evacuated as flood waters poured in. One
man died when he was struck by lightning
and several others suffered serious burns.

...In Warwickshire, Hell's Angels and
other bikers dried out after their annual
rock festival at Long Marston airfield
was rocked by violent thunderstorms.
The camp site was flooded after rain
swept the village, north of Stratford-
upon-Avon. ...

1 If storms _____ (6) a place, the place is
affected by very high winds and bad weather.

2 Very heavy rain is described as _____ . (10)

3 Very heavy rain causes _____ (8): areas that
are usually dry are covered with water. In this
context, water can be used in the plural, and the
journalist talks about _____ (5) waters.

4 When people are asked to leave their houses by the
authorities, for example because of flooding, they
are _____ . (9)

5 During an electrical storm people, trees, and
buildings may be _____ (6) by lightning.

6 Lightning can _____ _____ (3,4) to
buildings, causing them to burn.

7 Lightning comes with _____ (7). Electrical
storms are also known as _____ (13).

8 Section 8 of the Dictionary entry for _____
(4) explains this word in relation to explosions and
earthquakes, and section 11 explains the same
word in relation to music.

Unit 8

Audience approval

Check the meanings of these words or expressions in the Dictionary. Then use them to complete the text below. (Each word or expression occurs once.)

a applause   f fans
b audience   g indoors
c booing   h open air
d catcalls   i performance
e cheering   j venue

The _____ (1) for an event is the place where it happens. A big rock concert may take place in front of tens of thousands of _____ (2) in the _____ (3).

Opera is increasingly presented out of doors, but is more usually performed _____ (4) in more intimate surroundings with a smaller _____ (5).

However, the ways that the audience shows its opinion of the _____ (6) are very similar.

_____ (7) and _____ (8) show approval; _____ (9) and _____ (10) indicate the opposite.

Going out and staying in

Choose the correct alternatives. The first one has been done for you.

Some people like the experience of going out to watch live *entertainment* / *leisures* / *spectacles* on *scene* / *scenery* / *stage*. They enjoy being part of an *assistance* / *audience* / *ovation*.

Others prefer *halting* / *resting* / *staying* in to watch television. People who watch a lot of television, perhaps restlessly *zapping* / *zipping* / *zopping* between *channels* / *chains* / *canals* with their *distant-controls* / *far-controls* / *remote controls*, are sometimes called *couch* / *settee* / *sofa* potatoes.

People who listen to a lot of music have a more positive image. Those who know a lot about music are music *buffaloes* / *buffers* / *buffs*. But these people can be *blurs* / *borers* / *bores*. So can those obsessed with their *hi-fi* / *high-figh* / *hite-fi* equipment, talking endlessly about their ohms and their watts, their *soundphones* / *headphones* / *listeners* and their *highspeakers* / *loudspeakers* / *outspeakers*.

Frequent word: make

Look at the Dictionary entry for **make**. It has these sub-entries:

1 carrying out an action
2 causing or changing
3 creating or producing
4 link verb uses
5 achieving or reaching
6 stating an amount or time
7 phrasal verbs.

Which sub-entry does each example illustrate?

a She, who had always needed ten hours of sleep, now made do with five.

(__)

b I just wanted to make a comment about Prince Charles's comments.

(__)

c Volkswagen already makes cars in Spain.

(__)

d I made him look stupid in front of his friends.

(__)

e Actual hospital experience was a very good thing. I would have made a good doctor.

(__)

f Having finally made it back to Calais, he faced another long wait.

(__)

g The thief made off with jewellery worth £100,000.

(__)

h What time do you make it?

(__)

i He couldn't make it this evening because of work.

(__)

j What is the name of the outer layer of the Earth's atmosphere that is made up of hydrogen and helium?

(__)

k Do I make myself clear? Let me just explain.

(__)

l The politicians are just on the make.

(__)

Grammatical context: conjunctions

Look at the Dictionary entries for these conjunctions and phrasal conjunctions, labelled CONJ and PHR-CONJ in the Dictionary, and use them to complete the examples. (Each item occurs once.)

a even if   e providing
b however   f rather than
c in order to   g unless
d nor   h whereas

1 This is a collection of the English of the 1990s which we will analyse _____ find out how people actually use English.

2 The Red Cross has access to the prison, _____ it does not discuss conditions there.

3 They can understand English _____ they can't speak it themselves.

4 I gave up smoking. _____ , I have started again after 12 years.

5 There the children didn't know who they were or who they belonged to _____ here they know very well who they are.

6 Change could come from the bottom up, _____ the top down.

7 You can't learn more _____ you practise.

8 I'm neither for _____ against the Royal Family, but I wish they'd leave them alone.

Bygone phrases

Check the meanings of these words or expressions in the Dictionary.
Then use them to complete the examples below.

a bygone   e old-time
b Dark ages   f water under the bridge
c golden age   g yesteryear
d olden

1 Everyone wants pupils to write accurately, but returning to the methods of _____ is not the answer.

2 Arletty was to last into the Sixties, but she belonged to the _____ of French cinema, the 1930s and 1940s, when masterpieces flowed effortlessly from the Paris studios.

3 He's from a _____ age, an old soldier for whom honour is everything.

4 Can you imagine a society without technology? I think we'd be living in the _____ without all this.

5 It's easy to look at the situation and say, we might have done this, or might have done that, but it's all _____ now.

6 In the _____ days, the girls were married young.

7 'What sort of music do your mum and dad like best?' ' _____ music.'

Everything in common but their language 3

Find the equivalents of these terms relating to food in the other variety of English.
The first one has been done for you.

British English	American English
aubergine	eggplant
biscuit	
	flatware
fridge	
	jelly
joint	
mince	
	scallion
swede	
treacle	

Confusable verbs

Check the alternatives a–c in the Dictionary and complete the sentences correctly.

1 If you go to a lecture, you
   a attend it
   b assist it
   c give it.

2 If you recount a joke or a story, you
   a say it
   b speak it
   c tell it.

3 If an event is organized for a particular date and it is then decided that it should take place at a later date, it is
   a cancelled
   b postponed
   c brought forward.

4 If you succeed in an exam, you
   a pass it
   b take it
   c sit it.

5 If you take action to stop something from happening, you
   a avoid it
   b evade it
   c prevent it.

6 When you are dressed in your clothes, you are
   a carrying them
   b wearing them
   c apparelling them.

7 If you take something from someone without their permission, you
   a rob it
   b steal it
   c thieve it.

8 If you get money for doing a job, you
   a earn it
   b win it
   c gain it.

Stress in compounds 2

Look up these words in the Dictionary and find the odd one out from the point of view of stress.

sidearm	side-effect	sidelong
sideboard	side issue	side-on
sideburns	sidekick	side-saddle
sidecar	sidelight	sideshow
side dish	sideline	sidewalk

Words in context

Read this article from *Today* and answer the questions.

Egg theft birdman is caged

by Ian Gallagher

A bird dealer who bought stolen falcon eggs was jailed for four months yesterday.

Peter Gurr, 54, reared and sold the rare birds for profit, pretending they were bred in captivity when really they were taken from a nest in Scotland.

He was caught after the biggest-ever police operation against the trade.

Officers were alerted by bird experts suspicious of the number of chicks he was selling through *Cage and Aviary* magazine.

Police then traced the falcons he had sold to unsuspecting breeders all over Britain for between £250 and £700. They used DNA tests to prove that they had not been bred from captive birds. ...

1 A dealer is someone who b _ _ _ _ and s _ _ _ _ _ things.

2 Falcons are birds of p _ _ _ _ , and sometimes used for h _ _ _ _ _ _ _ .

3 Is **rear** pronounced the same as **rare**?

4 What is the base form of **bred**?

5 What word is used instead of **bred** in the example in the Dictionary entry for **captivity**?

6 What trade?

7 Is it possible to alert someone to a good situation?

8 Is a chick the same as a chicken?

9 If you are suspicious of an activity you s _ _ _ _ _ _ t something bad. If you are unsuspecting, you are not aware of something, but is it necessarily something bad?

10 If you trace something you find out where it came f _ _ _ .

11 What does DNA stand for? What type of DNA test is mentioned in the Dictionary?

Unit 9

Game of two halves

1 British people usually call this sport football. What do Americans call it and why?

2 The player with the ball is about to
  a fire
  b shoot
  c goal.

3 The man with a whistle is the
  a referee
  b judge
  c umpire.

4 The people watching are
  a spectators
  b watchers
  c lookers on.

5 Is there a capacity crowd?

Ballpark figures

1 How many players are there in a baseball team?

2 The four corners of the square are called
  a apexes
  b bases
  c wickets.

3 Do Americans call this a baseball pitch?

4 Which meaning of **pitcher** in the Dictionary does the drawing illustrate?

5 The player on the right is about to try to hit the ball with a
  a bat
  b club
  c stick.

Marathon men

1 Is this a field event?

2 The runners are running a
a course
b race
c game.

3 They are running on a
a course
b track
c circuit.

4 Number 358 is
a out in front
b out in a front
c out on the front.

5 You can refer to someone's past
performance, not just in athletics,
as their track r _ _ _ _ _ .

Punch-drunk

1 The man in a bow tie is the
a adjudicator
b referee
c arbiter.

2 He and the boxers are in the
a square
b rink
c ring.

3 If someone is KO'd, they are knocked
u n _ _ _ _ _ _ _ _ _ s .

4 If the boxers keep fighting until the
end of the match, they
a do the distance
b go the distance
c fight the distance.

5 Are the expressions **on the ropes**,
below the belt, and **throw in the towel**
only used in boxing?

Frequent word: way

Look at the Dictionary entry for **way**. All these examples contain **way**. Which numbered section of the entry for **way** does each example illustrate? (The examples here relate to the first ten sections. Each example illustrates a different section.)

a They are telling me in a nice way that I shouldn't be in the church.

(___)

b I don't know if you've ever been to San Francisco: it's very similar in many ways.

(___)

c I love the way you call people 'flower'.

(___)

d I turned on the TV to see which way the elections would go.

(___)

e 'I have nothing to do with the rest of the fashion business in Paris. I can do it my way,' she says.

(___)

f The machines help in several ways.

(___)

g I was worried about whether I'd be a good mother. I don't feel that way now.

(___)

h Japan is having to adjust to the ways of the rest of the world.

(___)

i 'So he's a hero?' 'That's one way of looking at it.'

(___)

j Anything that is really important and true can be expressed in a way that anyone can understand.

(___)

Grammatical context: numbers

Look in the Dictionary at the information on numbers, dates, and time on pages 1311 to 1314. Which of the examples below relate to:

a buildings	c people's ages	e sport
b dates	d quantity	f time

1 ...poetry written in the fifteen-eighties and published in the fifteen-nineties.

2 It doesn't matter if it's one-nil or two-nil.

3 Nobody in the late sixties and seventies was in business.

4 She looks ten years younger than most women in their late forties.

5 I'll come round at half three and we'll take it from there.

6 You may not know how to fix a broken pre-nineteen sixty eight Rolls Royce when in Tashkent, Uzbekistan.

7 I hadn't really got the idea that suite fifteen-o-five meant I'm on the fifteenth floor.

8 I looked at my clock radio and it was about twenty to three.

9 I get through twenty to twenty-five a day.

10 It's frightening that someone so young can be so good. I think she's ranked twelfth in the world.

What's cooking?

Check the expressions in bold in the Dictionary and complete the sentences.

1 If, in a discussion, you say that you want to put an issue on the **back burner**, you mean that you
   a will return to it later
   b want people to forget about it
   c accept that you have been wrong about it.

2 If you say that something makes your **blood boil**, it makes you very
   a angry
   b hot
   c excited.

3 If someone **cooks up a story**, they
   a make a story more interesting
   b tell a true story
   c invent a story.

4 If you describe someone or something as **flavour of the month**, you think that their popularity will
   a last a long time
   b not last a long time
   c return in a later month.

5 If you say that a plan is **half-baked**, you mean that
   a half of it is alright
   b it is half-way towards completion
   c it has not been thought out properly.

6 If you **spice up** a story, you
   a invent it completely
   b tell a story in a boring way
   c add interesting details to an existing story.

7 If you say that a plan has been **watered down**, you are saying that it has been changed
   a in a bad way
   b in a good way
   c in a way that leaves it basically the same.

Dated people

All the words below are labelled DATED in the Dictionary. Put them in the following groups:

1 words relating to jobs and professions, or a lack of one

2 words relating to character and intelligence

3 words relating to being married.

	group		group		group
aviator		numbskull		spinster	
betrothed		parson		suitor	
cobbler		retainer		usherette	
curmudgeon		sea dog		vagabond	
imbecile		sleuth		wench	

Trademark puzzle

All the numbered words below are identified as trademarks in the Dictionary.
Match each trademark to the category of product it refers to.

1 Crimplene	a cooking equipment
2 Dolby	b food
3 Jeep	c hi-fi equipment
4 Jell-O	d riot control equipment
5 Mace	e textiles
6 Primus	f tools
7 Stanley Knife	g vehicles

Same or different 2

Check the pronunciation of these pairs of words in the Dictionary. Look especially at different meanings, and pronunciation in British and American English. Are the underlined vowel sounds the same:

- always
- never
- sometimes: if so when?

Indicate this information in the table. The first one has been done for you.

	always	never	sometimes: when?
category / story			Pronounced the same in American English, but not in British English
food / should			
hostel / hostile			
leisure / seizure			
news / use			
nice / simultaneous			
privacy / private			
rude / dude			
tile / reptile			
tune / cartoon			

Words in context

Read this article from the *Independent* and answer the questions.

Parents warm to terms of 'pact'

Fran Abrams on a three-year 'deal' on pupil behaviour.

If a pupil at James Brindley High School in Stoke-on-Trent, Staffordshire, regularly fails to attend school, or is not properly dressed, his or her parents are likely to be reminded of the agreement they signed before their child arrived there.

The 800-pupil inner city comprehensive is one of a number which have already put into practice the plan for parent contracts advocated by Gillian Shephard, Secretary of State for Education.

Under a 'pact' introduced three years ago, parents are asked to sign a statement that they will send their children to school regularly, on time and properly dressed. They also agree to make sure that they have the right pencils and PE kit and do their homework properly, as well as promising to attend parents' meetings.

New arrivals at school agree to work quietly in class, bring pens, pencils and rulers and not to go out of school without permission. They must agree not to run down corridors, bang doors, shout or drop litter.

In return, the school agrees to provide regular homework, written reports, a newsletter and a wide range of extra-curricular activities.

1 Deals and pacts are kinds of
a _ _ _ _ m e n t .

2 Which section of the Dictionary entry for **pupil** is used here?

3 Someone who fails to attend school is a
t r u _ _ _ .

4 Is the school co-educational?

5 Do inner cities have a good reputation?

6 If you advocate something, do you recommend it?

7 Which section of the Dictionary entry for **Secretary of State** is used here?

8 Are statements always oral?

9 What does PE stand for?

10 If you do something properly, you do it
c _ _ _ _ _ _ l y .

11 Which section of the Dictionary entry for **arrival** is used here?

12 Are extra-curricular activities part of the normal classes?

Unit 10

Naming of parts

Label the drawing with these words.

cheek	eyelash
chin	forehead
ear	lips
eye	neck
eyebrow	shoulder

Label the drawing with these words.

ankle	knee
back	thigh
calf	toes
chest	wrist

Frequent word: do

Look at the Dictionary entry for **do**. It has these sub-entries:

1 auxiliary verb uses
2 other verb uses
3 noun uses.

Which sub-entry does each underlined example illustrate, and which numbered section does it relate to? (Each example illustrates a different section.)

a <u>Do</u> go ahead and record conversations if you want to.

(__ , __)

b <u>Does</u> she know you're going to do this?

(__ , __)

c What chemistry did you <u>do</u> at school and at university level?

(__ , __)

d <u>Don't</u> say anything in public.

(__ , __)

e Underwood plays for England, as <u>does</u> his brother.

(__ , __)

f I don't like a 15-minute break, and nor <u>do</u> the players.

(__ , __)

g I <u>do</u> the ironing and the washing.

(__ , __)

h Scientists are attempting to describe the world. Artists are trying to <u>do</u> the same thing.

(__ , __)

i What I should <u>do</u> is to invite him in for a cup of tea.

(__ , __)

j This system will <u>do</u> nothing to make the trains run on time.

(__ , __)

Grammatical context: pronouns

Check the Dictionary for the correct pronouns to complete these extracts. Each pronoun occurs once.

a anybody   f one
b everything   g somebody
c her   h something
d herself   i theirs
e none   j themselves

1 There seemed to be _____ wrong with the phone.

2 The writer made the point that it's OK for women to criticize _____ and laugh at themselves.

3 Our approach would be quite different from _____ .

4 The problem about character is that _____ can never as an actor understand all that a character is.

5 I've seen a few beggars in Paris but _____ to compare with the beggars and homeless I've seen in London.

6 It's amazing how she's grown since I last saw _____ .

7 If everybody had to mind their own business instead of _____ else's, there would be no war.

8 If _____ walks in with a cigarette, the fire alarm goes off.

9 She's well able to take care of _____ .

10 I hope that _____'s going to be alright.

Almost typical English expressions

The expressions in inverted commas are not quite right. Check them in the Dictionary and correct them.

1 If you 'keep your head above the wall', you avoid getting into difficulty.

2 If you 'see eye on eye' with someone, you agree with them.

3 If someone says that they are 'all ear', they mean that they are eager and ready to listen.

4 If you say that someone or something 'breaks your nose', you mean that they annoy you.

5 If you say that someone is 'breathing up your neck', you mean that they are watching you very closely.

6 If you say that someone 'received something on the chin', you mean that they accepted an unpleasant situation without making a lot of fuss.

7 If you say something 'tongue in the cheek', you make a remark that is ironic and not serious, even though it may seem serious.

8 If you 'let your hair go down', you relax completely and enjoy yourself.

9 If you say that someone is 'lying into their teeth', you are emphasizing that they are telling lies.

10 If you say that something is 'on the lips of everyone', you mean that a lot of people are talking about it.

Conventional responses

The expressions a–j are all labelled CONVENTION in the extra column of the Dictionary. Find them and then match them to the situations 1–10.

1 A politician leaves a meeting and is asked by journalists to say something, but the politician doesn't want to say anything. What does he or she say?

2 A friend is leaving on a long journey. What do you say to them?

3 You get to the station, intending to take the last train home, but someone tells you it has already left. What do you say to show you are not pleased about this?

4 Someone tells you they have bought a very expensive car. What do you say to show that you are not impressed?

5 Someone offers to carry your suitcase for you, but you tell them that you will carry it yourself.

6 You are watching a football match and someone scores a goal. You want to say that you are impressed.

7 Someone tells you about a friend going on holiday to an exotic place. You want to show that you envy them.

8 Someone asks you a question and you want to emphasize that you don't know the answer.

9 You hear on the news that England have lost again at cricket. What do you say to show your annoyance and disapproval?

10 You offer someone £3,000 for a car they are selling, and you want to say that you are definitely not prepared to pay more.

a Take it or leave it.

b Search me.

c No comment.

d Bon voyage.

e Nice one.

f I can manage.

g Big deal.

h You must be joking.

i Tut-tut.

j Lucky devil!

Prefix puzzle

Dis- is added to some words that describe processes, qualities, or states in order to form words describing the opposite processes, qualities, or states.

Mis- is added to some verbs and nouns to form new verbs and nouns which indicate that something is done badly or wrongly.

Complete the table, as in the first two examples. Indicate:
● the word class or classes of the word in the left column.
● if the word in the **Related word?** column is related to the word in the left column in one of the ways described above, or if it just does not exist at all.

	Word class			Related word?	yes	no	does not exist
	adj	verb	noun				
discard		✔		card		✔	
dishevelled	✔			hevelled			✔
disrespect				respect			
dissociate				sociate			
distrust				trust			
misadventure				adventure			
misanthrope				anthrope			
mischief				chief			
misgiving				giving			
mistrust				trust			

Schwa

Unstressed syllables are often pronounced /ə/. This sound is the same as the first vowel in 'about' and is called schwa. Underline the stressed syllables in these words and then put a line above the syllables pronounced /ə/.

1 conspirator / conspiratorial

2 contest (verb) / contest (noun)

3 future / futuristic

4 graduate (verb) / graduate (noun)

5 history / historical

6 imagination / imaginative

7 manager / managerial

8 obligation / obligatory

9 separate (adjective) / separated

10 tutor / tutorial

Words in context

Read this article from the *Guardian* and answer the questions.

The Burglar

by Duncan Campbell

Alec is, as he puts it, a 'self-employed businessman'. He gets up when he pleases, he dines well, he dresses well, takes holidays in Paris, Munich and Dublin, drives a BMW, entertains friends to nights out in the West End and travels home to Scotland for long weekends with his family. And three times a week he breaks into houses. For Alec is a burglar.

'My father was a welder who worked all his life and got nothing. He never went on holidays,' says Alec, now in his late 20s. 'I was a plasterer, but it's a mug's game. I want a bit more from life than that.'

He had done his first burglaries in Scotland, small-time affairs with mates who had cut up the settee of one victim. He did not approve. 'It's a waste of time messing up people's houses. I never do it – you don't get paid for it. I'm in and out in a maximum of 15 minutes.'

He lives in Southwark, South London, but after a couple of local break-ins he now concentrates on wealthier homes. His area is Chelsea, the King's Road, Fulham. He does a 'recce' by day and goes in through the window by night. Basements and houses with scaffolding outside are his favourites. He avoids houses with dogs – 'They're as frightened as you and they make too much noise.' ...

His favourite break-in time is two or three on a Sunday morning when the inhabitants will be sleeping soundly. 'I can usually get in the window – unless there's double glazing,' he says. 'You need to be a midget for that.' He ignores televisions and videos, concentrating on cheque books, credit cards or jewellery. 'You don't get much for a TV or video now anyway. It's only the desperadoes who go for them – the people who need to steal every day for drugs.' ...

1 Are self-employed people paid a salary by a firm?

2 Alec 'entertains friends to nights out in the West End'. Does this mean that he is an entertainer?

3 The crime of breaking into houses is called <u>b</u> <u>r</u> _ _ _ _ _ <u>y</u> .

4 Which sections of the entries for **mug** and **affair** in the Dictionary are these examples of? Where in the Dictionary is **small-time** defined?

5 If someone messes something up, they <u>s</u> _ _ _ <u>l</u> it.

6 Is Southwark a wealthy area?

7 Is **recce** used in American English?

8 **Frightened** means <u>a</u> _ _ _ _ _ <u>d</u> , <u>a</u> _ _ _ _ _ _ <u>s</u>, or <u>n</u> _ _ _ _ _ _ <u>s</u> .

9 Does the Dictionary refer to double glazing as a good way to prevent burglaries?

10 Is it normally acceptable to refer to someone as a 'midget'?

11 Do desperadoes worry about the danger of what they do?

Answer Key

UNIT 1

What to wear

1 No, only the one on the left is.
2 No, only the one on the right is.
3 No, only the one on the right is.
4 No, only the one on the right is.
5 No, only the one on the left is.
6 Yes, they both are.

Formal and casual

1a, 2b, 3b, 4c, 5b, 6a, 7c

Formal and formal

1 **Evening dress** consists of the formal clothes that people wear to formal occasions in the evening. This is the same as **evening wear**. An **evening dress** is a special dress that a woman wears to a formal occasion in the evening. Men can wear evening dress.
2 Yes
3 Yes
4 No, he is **holding** a glass.
5 b
6 a

Casual and casual

1 No, he is **wearing** headphones.
2 b
3 c
4 c
5 b

Frequent word: the

a 1	e 5	i 6
b 10	f 7	j 4
c 9	g 3	k 14
d 8	h 16	l 17

Grammatical context: uncount nouns

1 Can you give me any advice on what to do with it?
2 The company makes everything from aircraft to furniture and clothes.
3 We've got new uniforms and new equipment. Everything works.
4 Have you got any information on accommodation in Dublin or Ireland?
5 'I would not like to have been in the traffic.' 'No, I prefer to stay at home.'

6 I look on a car as just a way of getting from A to B. It's just a piece of machinery. It's a box on wheels.
7 Anyone with technical knowledge in the area could have thought of it.
8 American children spend less time in class and do less homework than Japanese children.
9 I saw in the press what I thought was good news.
10 NOTICE TO PASSENGERS. Only one piece of hand baggage allowed inside the aircraft.

Creature expressions

1b, 2a, 3e, 4f, 5d, 6g, 7c

Hey guys

	man / woman	formal / informal	British / American
big shot	both	informal	both
bloke	man	informal	British
chap	man	informal	British
character	both	informal	both
guy	man	informal	both
guys	both	informal	American
individual	both	—	both
personage	both	formal	both

Opposites or what?

	Word class			Opposite?	yes	no	does not exist
	adj	adv	noun				
inadequate	✓			adequate	✓		
infamous	✓			famous		✓	
innovation			✓	novation			✓
inaugural	✓			augural			✓
incessantly		✓		cessantly			✓
increment			✓	crement			✓
indolent	✓			dolent			✓
inflammable	✓			flammable		✓	
influx			✓	flux		✓	
innately		✓		nately			✓
invaluable	✓			valuable		✓	

Stress and word class 1

1 If Mexico cannot export its goods, it will export its people.
2 America's imports have been falling and its exports booming.
3 There is no tax on exports and the transport of imports.
4 A master wrote in my school report: 'Teaching this boy is a nightmare.'
5 More than 535 navigation 'incidents' were reported to the Department of Transport last year.

Words in context

1 a and c
2 No, it would be dated.
3 jewelry
4 duke
5 ladies-in-waiting
6 c

7 **Thought**: think, section 2; **hold**: hold, sub-entry 1, section 11
8 No. An heirloom is an object that has been in a family for a very long time.
9 Turn, sub-entry 1, section 21
10 Meetings, funerals, schools, colleges, churches, opera
11 Rockets, missiles, satellites, ships, lifeboats, military attacks, offensives, coups, campaigns, new products, services

UNIT 2

Mountain scenery

1b, c, d; 2a; 3b, d; 4a, b, c; 5b

Features of the landscape

1c, 2b, 3a, 4b, 5a, 6c

Frequent word: a/an

a	1	f	6
b	8	g	4
c	11	h	3
d	5	i	2
e	7	j	9

Grammatical context: verb patterns 1

1 His doctor advised him to retire as soon as possible.
2 At this point a large dog entered the room and was told it was not yet lunchtime.
3 Why do you say you hate shopping?
4 I think I'd like to go home.
5 The Slovaks like wine. The Czechs prefer beer.
6 The doctor can take these things away, but you can't prevent them coming back. *or*
The doctor can take these things away, but you can't prevent them from coming back.
7 Would you recommend that all first-year students live on campus? *or*
Would you recommend that all first-year students should live on campus?
8 I have yet to succeed in making good porridge.
9 I think smokers should respect non-smokers.

Under the weather

1b: **storm**, section 9
2a: **snowed under**, separate entry
3a: **rain check**, separate entry
4b: **foggy**, section 2
5c: **cloud**, section 8

The gift of the gab

1 articulate, eloquent, fluent; articulate
2 verbose, wordy
3 loquacious
4 loquacious
5 windbag
6 the gift of gab

Sub-entry puzzle

1 a: 1,6;	b: 2,3;	c: 2,1
2 a: 1,2;	b: 2,2;	c: 1,3
3 a: 1,7;	b: 2,2;	c: 3,1
4 a: 1,2;	b: 2,1;	c: 2,5
5 a: 1,3;	b: 2,1;	c: 2,6

Same spelling, different pronunciations

1 ...**lead**-free petrol. (red)
...**lead** such an exciting life. (heed)
2 ...a **bow**-tie. (hoe)
...**bow** your head in prayer. (cow)
3 ...a **row** of teeth. (know)
...so that the married couple can have a **row**. (now)
4 ...**tears** to his eyes. (fears)
...to **tear** up a professional contract. (rare)
5 ...to **wind** back the clock to a year ago. (signed)
...the music of **wind** in the trees. (binned)

Words in context

1 The first syllable	6 warning
2 No	7 Yes
3 The first	8 No
4 cut	9 No
5 across, up	10 The second

UNIT 3

Possible urban combinations

downtown ✓   ~~sidetown~~   ~~centretown~~   ~~off-town~~
tower block ✓   ~~blocktower~~   ~~house block~~   office block ✓
~~hanging bridge~~   ~~hung bridge~~   ~~suspended bridge~~   suspension bridge ✓
high street   ~~fly road~~   ~~down road~~   elevated highway ✓
aerodrome   airfield   airport ✓   airstrip
dockland ✓   quayside ✓   ~~quayhouse~~   warehouse

The places with ticks beside them above are in the picture.

Olde Worlde charm

This is a *view* over the *roofs* of an old town. The town looks *medieval*. The church has a tall *tower* with a *spire* on top. In the *background*, there are trees and other churches.

There are two main streets and off these run smaller, narrow *winding* streets. In one of the main streets, there is a traffic *jam*. This street suffers a lot from traffic *congestion*. In the other, traffic is *banned* and *pedestrians* can go shopping without the danger of being run over. But *parking* is difficult, and some people prefer to do their shopping *out of town*.

Frequent word: be

a 1,2	f 1,5
b 1,6	g 2,9
c 2,13	h 2,6
d 2,5	i 2,10
e 1,3	j 2,2

Grammatical context: phrasal verb patterns

1 People are free to choose how to bring up their children.
People are free to choose how to bring them up.
People are free to choose how to bring their children up.
2 The police had to check out the call.
The police had to check it out.
The police had to check the call out.
3 The agriculture minister has tried to explain away the scandal.
The agriculture minister has tried to explain it away.
The agriculture minister has tried to explain the scandal away.
4 We flagged down the tractor and climbed aboard.
We flagged it down and climbed aboard.
We flagged the tractor down and climbed aboard.
5 I'll never be able to give up smoking.
I'll never be able to give it up.
I'll never be able to give smoking up.
6 I marked down the number on a scrap of paper.
I marked it down on a scrap of paper.
I marked the number down on a scrap of paper.
7 They narrowed down the choice to about a dozen sites.
They narrowed it down to about a dozen sites.
They narrowed the choice down to about a dozen sites.
8 The enemy claimed to have shot down 22 of our planes.
The enemy claimed to have shot them down.
The enemy claimed to have shot 22 of our planes down.
9 Women need to weigh up the risks.
Women need to weigh them up.
Women need to weigh the risks up.

Watery phrases

1f, 2g, 3e, 4d, 5c, 6b, 7a

Everything in common but their language 1

British English	American English
car park	parking lot
caretaker	*janitor*
lift	elevator
ground floor	first floor
flat	*apartment*
tap	*faucet*
cupboard	closet
curtains	drapes
estate agent	*realtor*
burgle	burglarize

What is there to see?

	countryside	landscape	scenery	seascape
What you can see around you in a town		✓		
What you can see around you in the country	✓	✓	✓	
Theatre equipment			✓	
A type of painting		✓		✓
All the features that are important in a particular situation		✓		
What people do to land to create a pleasing effect		✓		

Unlikely couples

1 banned
2 blue
3 court
4 flower
5 guest
6 horse
7 keys
8 pear
9 roar

Words in context

1 Yes
2 abandon
3 alone
4 To be the first person to walk across Antarctica unaided
5 No
6 1 and 2
7 9
8 The second
9 b
10 properly
11 Yes

UNIT 4

Vehicle jungle

coach ✓
convertible ✓
double-decker
estate car ✓ B
hansom cab
hatchback
limousine ✓
lorry ✓ B
moped ✓
motorbike ✓
mountain bike ✓
penny farthing B
push bike ✓ B, D
saloon car ✓ B
scooter ✓
sports car ✓
van ✓

Out of control

1 planes, cars
2 planes, ships
3 cars
4 trains
5 ships
6 cars

Frequent word: of

a 2	d 11	g 7	j 3
b 1	e 10	h 4	k 12
c 6	f 14	i 16	l 17

Grammatical context: plurals

singular	plural	singular	plural	singular	plural
aircraft	*aircraft*	leaf	*leaves*	spacecraft	*spacecraft*
criterion	*criteria*	passer-by	*passers-by*	thief	*thieves*
foot	*feet*	phenomenon	*phenomena*	tomato	*tomatoes*
goose	*geese*	potato	*potatoes*	tooth	*teeth*
hanger-on	*hangers-on*	sheep	*sheep*	wolf	*wolves*

Group 1	Group 2	Group 3
aircraft *sheep* *spacecraft*	*criterion* *phenomenon*	*foot* *goose* *tooth*
Why? *Plural same as singular.*	Why? *Some words ending in '-on' take plural ending '-a'.*	Why? *Plural formed by changing vowel from 'oo' to 'ee'.*

Group 4	Group 5	Group 6
hanger-on *passer-by*	*potato* *tomato*	*leaf* *thief* *wolf*
Why? *Plural formed by adding 's' to first part of compound.*	Why? *Some words ending in '-o' form plural by adding '-es'.*	Why? *Some words ending in 'f' form plural by replacing '-f' with '-ves'.*

Approving and disapproving of people

apathetic D	philistine D
brash D	pompous D
cool-headed A	simple-minded D
dynamic A	strong-minded A
easy-going A	sulky D
modest A	tactful A
narcissistic D	thoughtful A
obsequious D	

Work puzzle

1 No	5 No
2 No	6 No
3 Yes	7 No
4 6	8 No

Stress and word class 2

1 conduct	5 contested
2 conflict	6 Contrast
3 conscript	7 convert
4 construct	8 convict

Words in context

1 snakes, lizards, crocodiles	6 cattle
2 6	7 No
3 box	8 hold
4 children	9 load
5 4	10 Customs and Excise

UNIT 5

Dream homes

1c, 2g, 3h, 4f, 5i, 6b, 7d, 8e, 9j, 10a

The homes in the picture are, from left to right:
a cottage, terraced houses, a bungalow, semis, and
a detached house.

An estate agent speaks

1 False: the building has four floors and a sloping roof.
2 False: only the flat on the first and second floors is on two floors.
3 False: only the flat on the top floor has a balcony.
4 True
5 False: they are all furnished.
6 False: there are people living in the top flat.
7 False: the front door opens directly into the living room on the ground floor and the first floor.
8 True
9 False: there are no curtains in the kitchen on the ground floor and first floor.
10 False: the staircase leads up to a landing between the bedroom and the bathroom.

Frequent word: and

a 3	c 1	e 5	g 9	i 11
b 6	d 4	f 10	h 2	j 7

Grammatical context: adjectives

	group		group		group
ablaze	2	affable	1	ambidextrous	2
abnormal	1	afraid	1	amphibious	2
absent	3	alight	2	anatomical	2
adrift	3	alive	3	asleep	2
advisable	1	alone	3	awake	1

Disaster area

1d, 2a, 3c, 4e, 5g, 6b, 7f

Literary people

1b, 2f, 3e, 4g, 5c, 6j, 7a, 8i, 9h, 10d

Talking about the future

1 The marriage of Alix and Bertie appeared to be on the brink of disaster.
2 There's every chance that something better will be around the corner if she does the sensible thing.
3 Was there no good news on the horizon?
4 A final victory over the Mafia is possible. Possible, maybe, but not imminent.
5 Are you going to get a computer in the near future?
6 The huge factory was on the point of beginning production of one million television sets.
7 Those changes still seem a long way away.

Fertile exercise

Group 1	Group 2	Group 3
adult amateur laboratory moustache	fertile futile hostile volatile	institute nude numerical tune
Why? These words have different stress patterns in British and American English.	Why? The final syllable of these words is pronounced /tail/ in British English and /təl/ in American English.	Why? The 'u' sound of these words is pronounced / juː/ in British English and /uː/ in American English.

Words in context

1 No: the word does not exist	9 greedy
2 shopping	10 happen
3 No	11 miles per hour
4 23	12 No
5 No	13 No
6 No	14 spokesperson
7 develops	15 Yes
8 1	16 threat
	17 No

UNIT 6

True, false, or worse?

1 Impossible from the language point of view: **furniture** is an uncount noun and so cannot be used in the plural.
2 Grammatical, but not true.
3 Grammatical and true.
4 True, but **rug** is mis-spelled.
5 Impossible from the language point of view: these are **armchairs** or **easy chairs**.
6 Impossible from the language point of view: these are **dining chairs** and a **dining table**.
7 Impossible from the language point of view: **equipment** is an uncount noun and so cannot be used in the plural, and the plural of **shelf** is **shelves**.
8 True
9 Impossible from the language point of view. This should be: 'The rug has a fringe around its edge.'
10 Impossible from the language point of view: you cannot put **to** after **opposite** in this sentence.

Design for living

The room is ...	Living room	Kitchen	The room is ...	Living room	Kitchen
a dump		✓	~~impeccable~~		
a mess		✓	neat	✓	
a pigsty		✓	~~ordered~~		
a tip		✓	orderly	✓	
clean	✓		smart	✓	
~~clean-cut~~			tidy	✓	
disorganized		✓	~~well-dressed~~		
immaculate	✓		~~workmanlike~~		

Frequent word: that

a 1,1   d 2,2   g 1,7   i 1,15
b 1,4   e 1,11   h 1,13   j 1,14
c 2,4   f 1,10

Grammatical context: adverbs

	adverb	adjective
awfully	✓	
comely		✓
fast	✓	✓
friendly		✓
hard	✓	✓
hardly	✓	
heavenly		✓
homely		✓
incredibly	✓	
motley		✓
perfectly	✓	
prettily	✓	
quarterly	✓	✓
really	✓	
reasonably	✓	

Colourful expressions

The odd one out is **yellow flower** because it means a flower that is yellow and nothing else. All the other expressions have special meanings: see headwords.

Jargon jungle

1k, 2e, 3a, 4g, 5b, 6j, 7c, 8h, 9i, 10f, 11d

Confusable adjectives

1a, 2a, 3c, 4a, 5c, 6b, 7c, 8c, 9b, 10b

Stress in compounds 1

	first syllable stressed	first and second syllables stressed
backcloth	✓	
backcomb		✓
backdate		✓
back door		✓
backfire		✓
background	✓	
backhander	✓	
backlash	✓	
back pedal		✓
backstroke	✓	
backtrack	✓	
backup	✓	

Words in context

1 No
2 17
3 No, they talk about **checking in**.
4 No
5 No, **suspect** does not have this meaning as an adjective.
6 steal
7 No
8 2
9 Yes
10 4
11 No

UNIT 7

The usual suspects

1d, 2e, 3c, 4f, 5a, 6b

Frequent word: have

a 1,1	f 3,3
b 1,5	g 3,9
c 1,3	h 3,7
d 2,1	i 3,13
e 3,1	j 4,1

Grammatical context: verb patterns 2

1 Yes	7 No
2 No	8 No
3 Yes	9 No
4 Yes	10 Yes
5 Yes	11 Yes
6 No	12 No

Questions of life

	headword
double life	separate headword: **double life**
get a life	**life** 21
kiss of life	separate headword: **kiss of life**
larger than life	**life** 35
life and soul of the party	**life** 11
long-life	separate headword: **long-life**
shelf life	separate headword: **shelf life**
still life	separate headword: **still life**
That's life	**life** 33
the time of your life	**time** 71

Confusable nouns

1b, 2b, 3c, 4c, 5b, 6c, 7a, 8a

Same or different 1

	always	never	sometimes: when?
bare / bear	✔		
deliberate / estimate			when they are both verbs, and when **deliberate** is an adjective and **estimate** a noun
head / read			when **read** is the past tense
kind / wind			when **wind** means turning or wrapping
now / sow			when **sow** means a female pig
paw / saw	✔		
pear / pier		✔	
realize / surprise	✔		

Words in context

1 batter
2 torrential
3 flooding, flood
4 evacuated
5 struck
6 set fire
7 thunder, thunderstorms
8 rock

Everything in common but their language 2

British English	American English
boot	trunk
bonnet	hood
estate car	station wagon
exhaust pipe	tailpipe
lorry	truck
petrol	gas, gasoline
saloon car	sedan
tyre	tire
windscreen	windshield
wing	fender

UNIT 8

Audience approval

1j, 2f, 3h, 4g, 5b, 6i, 7a, 8e, 9c, 10d

Going out and staying in

Some people like the experience of going out to watch live *entertainment* on *stage*. They enjoy being part of an *audience*.

Others prefer *staying* in to watch television. People who watch a lot of television, perhaps restlessly *zapping* between *channels* with their *remote controls*, are sometimes called *couch* potatoes.

People who listen to a lot of music have a more positive image. Those who know a lot about music are music *buffs*. But these people can be *bores*. So can those obsessed with their *hi-fi* equipment, talking endlessly about their ohms and their watts, their *headphones* and their *loudspeakers*.

Frequent word: make

a	1	g	7
b	1	h	6
c	3	i	5
d	2	j	7
e	4	k	2
f	5	l	3

Grammatical context: conjunctions

1c, 2e, 3a, 4b, 5h, 6f, 7g, 8d

Bygone phrases

1g, 2c, 3a, 4b, 5f, 6d, 7e

Everything in common but their language 3

British English	American English
aubergine	eggplant
biscuit	*cookie*
cutlery	flatware
fridge	*refrigerator*
jam	jelly
joint	*roast*
mince	*hamburger meat*
spring onion	scallion
swede	*rutabaga*
treacle	*molasses*

Confusable verbs

1a, 2c, 3b, 4a, 5c, 6b, 7b, 8a

Stress in compounds 2

The odd one out is **side-on** because it is stressed on two syllables, whereas all the others are only stressed on the first syllable.

Words in context

1 buys, sells
2 prey, hunting
3 No
4 breed
5 reared
6 The illegal trade in birds' eggs
7 No
8 No
9 suspect; No
10 from
11 deoxyribonucleic acid; DNA fingerprinting

UNIT 9

Game of two halves

1 Soccer, to distinguish it from American football; 2b; 3a; 4a; 5 Yes

Ballpark figures

1 9; 2b; 3 No, a baseball field; 4 pitcher, section 3; 5a

Marathon men

1 No, a track event; 2b; 3b; 4a; 5 record

Punch-drunk

1b; 2c; 3 unconscious; 4b; 5 No

Frequent word: way

a	2	f	3
b	4	g	9
c	10	h	5
d	8	i	7
e	6	j	1

Grammatical context: numbers

1b, 2e, 3b, 4c, 5f, 6b, 7a, 8f, 9d, 10e

What's cooking?

1a, 2a, 3c, 4b, 5c, 6c, 7a

Dated people

	group		group		group
aviator	*1*	numbskull	*2*	spinster	*3*
betrothed	*3*	parson	*1*	suitor	*3*
cobbler	*1*	retainer	*1*	usherette	*1*
curmudgeon	*2*	sea dog	*1*	vagabond	*1*
imbecile	*2*	sleuth	*1*	wench	*1*

Trademark puzzle

1e, 2c, 3g, 4b, 5d, 6a, 7f

Same or different 2

	always	never	sometimes: when?
categ<u>o</u>ry / st<u>o</u>ry			*Pronounced the same in American English, but not in British English*
f<u>oo</u>d / sh<u>ou</u>ld		✓	
hos<u>t</u>el / hos<u>t</u>ile			*Pronounced the same in American English, but not in British English*
l<u>ei</u>sure / s<u>ei</u>zure			*Pronounced the same in American English, but not in British English*
n<u>ew</u>s / <u>u</u>se			*Pronounced the same in British English, but not in American English*
n<u>i</u>ce / simultane<u>ou</u>s			*Pronounced the same in American English, but not in British English*
pri<u>v</u>acy / pri<u>v</u>ate			*Pronounced the same in American English, but not in British English*
r<u>u</u>de / d<u>u</u>de			*Pronounced the same in American English, but not in British English*
t<u>i</u>le / rep<u>ti</u>le			*Pronounced the same in British English, but not in American English*
t<u>u</u>ne / cart<u>oo</u>n			*Pronounced the same in American English, but not in British English*

Words in context

1 agreement
2 I
3 truant
4 Yes
5 No
6 Yes
7 2
8 No
9 physical education
10 correctly
11 5
12 No

UNIT 10

Naming of parts

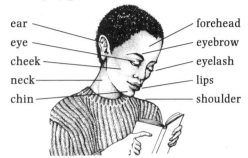

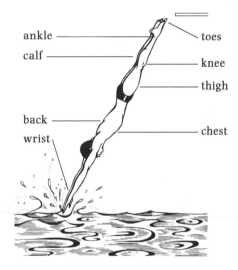

Frequent word: do

a 1,7
b 1,2
c 2,15
d 1,5
e 1,8
f 1,9
g 2,1
h 2,2
i 2,3
j 2,6

Grammatical context: pronouns

1h, 2j, 3i, 4f, 5e, 6c, 7g, 8a, 9d, 10b

Almost typical English expressions

1 If you **keep your head above water**, you avoid getting into difficulty.
2 If you see **eye to eye** with someone, you agree with them.
3 If someone says that they are **all ears**, they mean that they are eager and ready to listen.
4 If you say that someone or something **gets up your nose**, you mean that they annoy you.
5 If you say that someone is **breathing down your neck**, you mean that they are watching you very closely.
6 If you say that someone **took something on the chin**, you mean that they accepted an unpleasant situation without making a lot of fuss.
7 If you say something **tongue in cheek**, you make a remark that is ironic and not serious, even though it may seem serious.
8 If you **let your hair down**, you relax completely and enjoy yourself.
9 If you say that someone is **lying through their teeth**, you are emphasizing that they are telling lies.
10 If you say that something is **on everyone's lips**, you mean that a lot of people are talking about it.

Conventional responses

1c, 2d, 3h, 4g, 5f, 6e, 7j, 8b, 9i, 10a

Schwa

1 conspirator / conspiratorial
2 contest (verb) / contest (noun)
3 future / futuristic
4 graduate (verb) / graduate (noun)
5 history / historical
6 imagination / imaginative
7 manager / managerial
8 obligation / obligatory
9 separate (adjective) / separated
10 tutor / tutorial

Words in context

1 No
2 No
3 burglary
4 mug 3 and affair 1; small-time has its own headword
5 spoil
6 No
7 No
8 afraid, anxious, nervous
9 No
10 No: some people find this use offensive.
11 No

Prefix puzzle

	Word class			Related word?	yes	no	does not exist
	adj	verb	noun				
discard		✔		card		✔	
dishevelled	✔			hevelled			✔
disrespect			✔	respect	✔		
dissociate		✔		sociate			✔
distrust		✔	✔	trust	✔		
misadventure			✔	adventure	✔		
misanthrope			✔	anthrope			✔
mischief			✔	chief		✔	
misgiving			✔	giving		✔	
mistrust		✔	✔	trust	✔		